This boo gs to:

....

Editorship: Ana Delgado
Text supervision: Carole Patton
Academic support and advice: Carlota Arroyo,
Niko Domínguez
Layout and design: Estelle Talavera
Illustrations: Eva María Gey (story),
Cristina de Cos-Estrada (vocabulary and activities)

c/ Campezo, 13 - 28022 Madrid
Tel. 91 300 91 00 - Fax: 91 300 91 18
Impreso y encuadernado en España.
www.susaeta.com

Impreso en papel procedente de bosques sostenibles.

D.L.: M-19394-MMXX

EASY READING

An Absent-Minded Dinosaur

susaeta

TOTO IS A **DIPLODOCUS**.

HE HAS MANY FRIENDS
AND IS A HAPPY **DINOSAUR**.
BUT HE HAS A PROBLEM:
HE'S VERY **ABSENT-MINDED**!

HE **FORGETS** EVERYTHING...

FOR EXAMPLE:

HE **FORGETS** TO SET THE ALARM CLOCK WHEN HE GOES TO SLEEP.

"OH NO! I AM GOING TO BE LATE!"

"TAKE THIS **NOTEBOOK**", SAYS MUM.

"WRITE EVERYTHING YOU HAVE TO DO", SHE SAYS.

TOTO WRITES:

1. STUDY MATHS

2. DO HOMEWORK

3. TAKE A SNACK

HE WALKS TO
SCHOOL...
BUT HE FORGETS
HIS NOTEBOOK!

"CAN I PLAY WITH YOUR LITTLE T-REX?", TOTO ASKS HIS FRIEND ONE DAY.

"OK, BUT PLEASE, **DON'T LOSE IT!**", SAYS HE.

PROMISED!

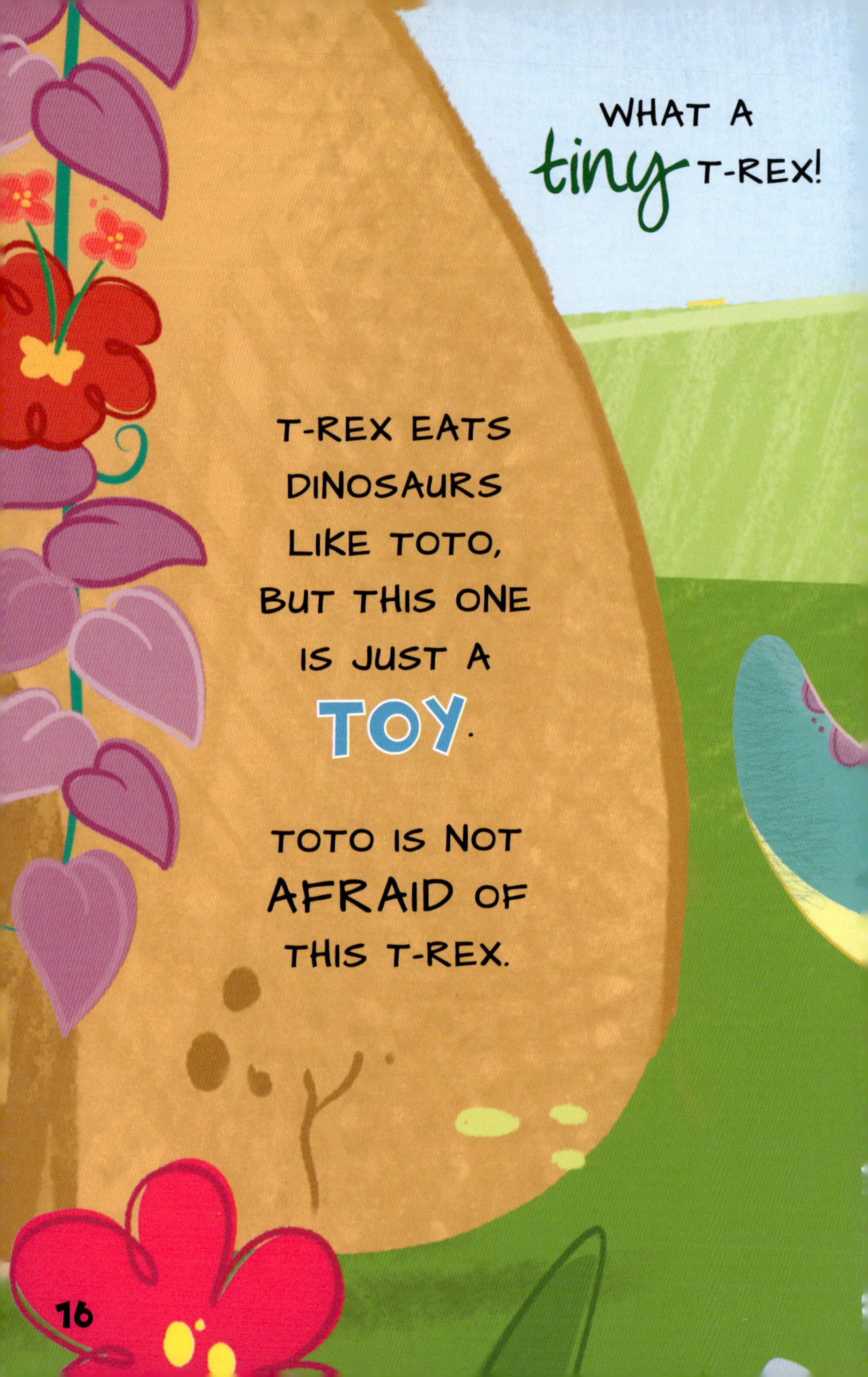

WHAT A *tiny* T-REX!

T-REX EATS DINOSAURS LIKE TOTO, BUT THIS ONE IS JUST A **TOY**.

TOTO IS NOT **AFRAID** OF THIS T-REX.

TOTO SHOWS THE T-REX TO HIS FRIENDS.

"LOOK AT IT!"

THEY ALL **LAUGH** ABOUT THE LITTLE DINOSAUR.

Ha ha ha!
Ha ha ha!

THEN THEY GO SWIMMING IN THE RIVER, AND TOTO **FORGETS** SOMETHING...

THE **TOY**!

"I LOVE PLAYING IN THE WATER! IT'S SO MUCH **FUN**!"

BUT LATER, TOTO CANNOT FIND THE T-REX.

AND SO HE **CRIES**.

SUDDENLY, A VOICE SAYS:
"WHY ARE YOU **CRYING**?"

IT'S A REAL T-REX!!!

TOTO IS SCARED.

IT'S A GIANT T-REX!

"DON'T BE AFRAID. I WANT TO HELP YOU. WHAT IS YOUR PROBLEM?", THE T-REX ASKS.

"I AM AN ABSENT-MINDED DINOSAUR", SAYS TOTO.

THE T-REX HELPS TOTO *FIND* THE **TOY**.

"NEXT TIME,
TIE A **STICK**
TO YOUR LEG.
IT WILL HELP YOU
REMEMBER WHAT
YOU HAVE TO DO!"

AND THAT IS
A GOOD IDEA!!!

THE END

VOCABULARY

ALARM CLOCK

SNACK

HOMEWORK

NOTEBOOK

MATHS

TOY

SCARED

MATCH THE OPPOSITES WITH ARROWS.

TINY

CRY

LOSE

GIANT

REMEMBER

FIND

LAUGH

FORGET

NUMBER THE IMAGES.

- [1] TOTO **FORGETS** TO SET THE **ALARM CLOCK**.
- [ ] HIS MUM GIVES TOTO A **NOTEBOOK**.
- [ ] THEY ALL **LAUGH** ABOUT THE LITTLE DINOSAUR.
- [ ] TOTO IS **SCARED** OF THE **GIANT** T-REX.

1

2

3

4